21 Days of Hope

An Intentional Journey
Toward Fullness in Christ

TIM PARSONS

21 Days of Hope: An Intentional Journey Toward Fullness in Christ

ISBN 978-1-7360063-1-3

Copyright © 2021 Tim Parsons

All rights reserved.

Published by Tim Parsons Leadership, 2021

No parts of this publication may be reproduced, stored in a retrieval system, or transmitted in any form or by any means, electronic, mechanical, photocopying, recording, or otherwise, without the prior written permission of the copyright owner.

This book is sold subject to the condition that it shall not, by way of trade or otherwise, be lent, resold, hired out, or otherwise circulated without the publisher's prior consent in any form of binding or cover other than that in which it is published and without similar condition including this condition being imposed on the subsequent purchaser. Under no circumstances may any part of this book be photocopied for resale.

Cover by Canva (canva.com)

S.O.A.P.© created by Pastor Wayne Cordeiro

Scripture quotations taken from the Holy Bible, New Living Translation, copyright ©1996, 2004, 2015 by Tyndale House Foundation. Used by permission of Tyndale House Publishers Inc., Carol Stream, Illinois 60188. All rights reserved.

DEDICATED TO:

The people of The Journey Church. Your heart for God and others has inspired me to follow your lead and not give up hope! You are an inspiration for our community and there are people coming to Christ who wouldn't have without the love you expressed. This book is really a culmination of what I've learned from you. Continue being blessed and being a blessing to those around you!

INTRODUCTION

In 2020, our world was hit with the coronavirus pandemic, and it altered life for a short period and for the long-term both. Like everyone else, I found myself wrestling with the emotional and spiritual effects of what we were all walking through. The temptation was to lose my hope.

The church that I lead went into quarantine and started having online-only services on Sundays and virtual small groups through the week. As we became more disconnected the feelings of loneliness and isolation grew stronger. Rather than allow ourselves to fall into a deep pit of despair, we committed together to journey toward 21 days of hope.

During this 21-day period, we read devotionals together and attempted to bring hope to our neighbors, friends, family, and co-workers. And that was the genesis of the devotional journey you're about to embark on. You'll notice some references to quarantine and the pandemic because we saw that as our greatest opportunity to find hope and bring hope.

So, as you read through these pages, it's my desire that you will feel hope well up in you. That the ways we attempted to find hope during the pandemic of 2020 will fill your life with the hope of Jesus Christ. Please know that these devotions are prayed over, and they are anointed with the Holy Spirit for your benefit and His glory.

Now, lean into these next 21 days. You're about to go on a journey that will bring hope to your life if you will not only read the words but allow them to penetrate your heart. And, as you are filled with hope, please be a hope-bringer to those around you. God bless you!

Timothy P. Parsons
LEADERSHIP FOR THE REST OF US

DAY ONE

Matthew 12:21 (NLT)

"And his name will be the hope of all the world."

I hardly ever carry cash. Maybe you're like me in that way. When I'm going somewhere that only accepts cash or I need a gift for one of my kids' friends' birthday parties, I have to plan ahead and go to the ATM first. There have been many occasions where I've needed cash only to find an empty pocket or a vacant billfold.

The same is true of hope. It is nearly impossible to give someone something that you do not have.

When Jesus came on the scene, he was met with a hopeless world. Much like today, people were looking for hope in money, relationships, position, intellect, and even religion. Little did they know that hope is found in the Name above all other names.

For you and me, if we want to bring hope to our community, we must first be hope-filled. The only way to do that is to allow Jesus to be our source. In other words, we cannot look to anything else as the reason for and the foundation of our hope. Because His Name is the HOPE of all the world – even ours!

Consider: Where does your hope come from?

Prayer: *"Father, please help me to look to Jesus daily as the source of my hope. As I desire to spread hope in my community, I pray that I would be filled with Your hope. In Jesus' name, amen."*

JOURNAL

DAY TWO

Romans 4:18 (NLT)

Even when there was no reason for hope, Abraham kept hoping—believing that he would become the father of many nations. For God had said to him, "That's how many descendants you will have!"

I don't know about you, but I had so many plans for 2020. Plans that I thought were God-given and God-ordained. Plans that were good and were for the good of others. Heading into that season, I was full of hope for what was next.

Then, we were quarantined. In one moment, everything changed. All of my plans were thrown out the window.

For all intents and purposes, it seemed as if I had no reason for hope. Ever been there? I found myself at times feeling down, confused, and even hopeless.

But I was reminded as we are today that, with God, there is always a reason to be full of hope. Why? Because of His promises to us! No matter how things look around us, His promises are always "yes and amen"!

And, if I may, can I encourage you to be the father or mother of many "nations"? Here's what I mean by that: You and I are to have "offspring" of people who carry our DNA of hope in Jesus Christ. We are to give birth to others who are full of hope – even when there seems to be no reason for hope! We have been positioned, gifted, and empowered by God to bring hope to a broken world!

In what ways have your thoughts or actions communicated that there is "no reason for hope"? How can you "give birth" to descendants who are full of hope in Jesus Christ?

Prayer: *"God, I pray that you would show me the areas of my life that lack hope. Help me to find the hopefulness in all situations. I pray that I will see divine opportunities today to bring hope to a broken world. In Jesus' name, amen."*

JOURNAL

DAY THREE

Romans 5:4 (NLT)

And endurance develops strength of character, and character strengthens our confident hope of salvation.

Some situations, like exercising, we can give up on easily and walk away. Other situations, like a global pandemic, not so much. But both hold the promise of a better tomorrow if we will endure through them. I find in myself, however, that perseverance is often in short supply. I struggle to keep going, especially when it's hard.

Our faith is the same. We are instructed to endure, to persevere, to keep going. And, on the other side of that lies a better tomorrow – one that's full of HOPE. Truth be told, we all are faced with giving up on our faith regularly. And we probably give up on our faith more than we realize.

Some "giving up" is like exercising – it's in the small things. We get impatient waiting on what we believe God will and can do, so we do it ourselves (we take another job, we go deeper in debt, we jump into another relationship, and so on). Other times are like a global pandemic, when we are forced into situations that we did not choose and may not even agree with and we begin to question our faith altogether. Where is God? Why would God let this happen?

Ever been there? I know I have. But we are instructed to endure. To persevere. To push on and push through. Why? Because on the other side is HOPE. I have been through some very tough stuff in my life, and I have given up and I have endured. I can say with full confidence that the times I endured, I was able to find HOPE on the other side. And my character was built in the process. In other words, when I faced subsequent situations where I was faced with the option to give up or to keep going, it became easier for me to trust God.

What area(s) of your life is God asking you to endure through so you can see His hope at a deeper level?

Prayer: *"Father, you are the God of hope. Help me to endure, especially when things are hard. I pray that my character would be built up so that I can see more clearly all the ways you provide for me. I give my problems, uncertainties, and worries over to you today. In Jesus' name, amen."*

JOURNAL

DAY FOUR

Romans 5:5 (NLT)

And this hope will not lead to disappointment. For we know how dearly God loves us, because he has given us the Holy Spirit to fill our hearts with his love.

God's love is the foundation of our hope. It's not anything we bring to the table, but everything that God is. God is love. And he "so loved" us that he sent Jesus to die for us. God's love is wider, longer, higher, deeper, more extravagant, and more complete than anything we can even imagine. God loves you.

I love my children deeply. But not as much as God loves them. I love my wife sincerely. But not as much as God loves her. I love my family unconditionally. But not as much as God loves them. I love all of you dearly. But not as much as God loves you.

Sometimes, we imagine that love is equal to being happy. We think that love extended toward us means that we will always be happy, content, and satisfied. And, the moment we don't feel those ways, we can easily suppose the other person doesn't love us. If we aren't careful, we can treat God the same way. When we do, that's when hopelessness can begin to set in. Ever been there?

There are two specific times I see this in my own life. When God is silent or when God closes a door (or says "no"). If I don't check my heart, I weave a story about God and how He doesn't love me because I didn't get what I want…or I'm not happy…or He didn't come through for me…etc. A sign of maturity for the believer is when God is silent or says "no" and we are able to trust Him anyway. At the root is a trust that He loves us and wants the best for us.

We see here that His love for us leads us to a hope that will not disappoint. If you have an area of your life that seems hopeless, find your way to God's love. If God is silent, lean into His love. If God has closed a door or said "no" to something, rest in His love. Allow the love of God to breathe hope into your life today.

In what ways have you seen God's love in a tangible way? How can you use that to help you in other areas of your life?

Prayer: *"God, I thank you that you love me. Your love brings hope, peace, and comfort into my heart and mind today. I pray that as I deal with hopeless areas of my life and as I extend hope to others, that your love would be my foundation. Help me to see it, feel it, and know it in a fresh way today. In Jesus' name, amen."*

JOURNAL

DAY FIVE

Romans 8:24 (NLT)
We were given this hope when we were saved.

Have you ever had a skill that seems to come easily for you? Maybe it's a hobby or you see it in your career. It could be something you do with your hands or the fact that math was easy for you. For me, it's teaching. For some reason, I am able to take something that is somewhat complicated to others and break it down into easy-to-understand chunks.

Teaching, although I can improve and get better at it over time, it comes "naturally." It's just "in me." Of course, I know without a shadow of a doubt that it's a gift given to me by God.

Hope works the same way. From the moment you're saved, it's in you. We all can (and should) get better over time at having hope – but it's not something you need to go searching for. It's in you!

The times when I feel like I don't do well at teaching are usually the times when I've over-thought it, leaned too much on my own intellect, or made the process much harder than it needed to be. Sound familiar? Yeah, we do the same thing with hope.

In other words, don't over-think it. Don't lean too much on your own intellect. And don't make the process harder than it needs to be. Afterall, it's in you. Hope was given to you when you were saved. Jesus is our hope…all we need to do is engage it (Him).

Was it easier to see God's hope now or when you were first saved? If you're like most of us, it was when you were first saved. But that doesn't mean it's any less "in you" than when you were first saved. Life, circumstances, worry, and even sin can drown out God's hope in us. Engage God's hope in His son Jesus Christ today!

Does hope come natural to you or do you find it's something you have to work at? What is one step you can take today to engage God's hope where you need it most?

Prayer: "Thank you for the hope you gave me when I was saved! You are full of grace for giving me such an amazing gift! Help me to find the hope that is in me each and every day. I pray that I would overflow with hope so that I can extend it to those I'm around. In Jesus' name, amen."

JOURNAL

_____
_____
_____
_____
_____
_____
_____
_____
_____
_____
_____
_____
_____
_____
_____

DAY SIX

Romans 12:12 (NLT)

Rejoice in our confident hope. Be patient in trouble, and keep on praying.

Rejoice! And again I say, Rejoice! I can just hear Paul's words echoing in my spirit. He writes those words to the Philippian church. Here, to the Roman church, he gets specific. Rejoice in our confident hope. In other words, the fact that we are confident in our hope in Jesus Christ should bring us great JOY! Have joy! And again I say, Have JOY!

He continues – "be patient in trouble…". Patience. It's one of the 3 words that I shared with you about re-launching our Sunday morning services. As a reminder they were be Patient, be Positive, and be People-focused. But, patience is directly tied to hope, isn't it? It's far easier to be patient when I know something good will come out of the waiting. The problem comes when I find myself in a hopeless place. It is far more difficult to wait patiently when I am unsure that any good will come out of my situation.

So, what do we do?

"Keep on praying." Keep on praying. Have you prayed as much as you've worried? Have you prayed as much as you've researched? Have you prayed as much as you've scrolled, commented, and posted on social media?

And here's what's true, praying doesn't always change our circumstances, but it does change us. Come on somebody! Read that again. Often our goal when we pray is for God to change something or someone, am I right? Rarely do we ever pray for God to change US. But I believe that just may be God's greatest work right now. "Oh God, change ME."

As He does His work in us, we will find – I'm sure of it – we will find a deeper sense of hope…which will lead us to a greater sense of JOY! Church, rejoice in your confident hope today!

Prayer: *"Father, thank you for the confident hope I have in Jesus Christ! Help me to rejoice in that truth every day. I pray that I would be patient in whatever trouble I may find myself in and that I would pray more than I worry. Today, I choose joy. In Jesus' name, amen."*

JOURNAL

DAY SEVEN

Romans 15:4 (NLT)

Such things were written in the Scriptures long ago to teach us. And the Scriptures give us hope and encouragement as we wait patiently for God's promises to be fulfilled.

I'm not sure there's a better verse for today! Feeling hopeless? Go to Scripture. Feeling discouraged? Go to Scripture. Getting tired of waiting? Go to Scripture.

Take a moment right now and read Romans 15:1-3. We need the context of what it's referring to when it says, "such things." I'll wait...

You see, Scripture is meant to be instructive, inspirational, and prophetic. We find instruction in there on how we are to live (verses one through three). Then, we find inspiration – hope and encouragement! Lastly, Scripture is prophetic. In other words, things we're written "long ago" that are meant to help us today.

There are no surprises to God. He provided for us "long ago" words that are meant give us hope and encouragement. Promises that will be fulfilled. Words that will breathe life into our mortal bodies.

As we gather to worship Him today, consider how Scripture will give you hope and encouragement as you wait patiently for His promises to be fulfilled. He will never leave, nor forsake you. All of his promises are yes and amen. He is near to the brokenhearted. If He is for us, who can be against us? Nothing can separate us from the love of God. His grace is sufficient for us. He says, come to me and I will give you rest. He has overcome the world!

In case you didn't catch it, those are all Scriptures. Find hope in them today.

Prayer: *"God, thank you for your Word. I pray that I will find hope and encouragement in it today. Open my eyes to how you are working in me through Scripture. In Jesus' name, amen."*

JOURNAL

DAY EIGHT

Romans 15:13 (NLT)
I pray that God, the source of hope, will fill you completely with joy and peace because you trust in him. Then you will overflow with confident hope through the power of the Holy Spirit.

Trust is an interesting thing, isn't it? Some people say that trust has to be earned. I don't necessarily agree with that. But I do think trust can be lost very quickly and can take a long time to rebuild. But there's a paradox when it comes to trust. In order to build trust, you have to trust. And the more you trust (and the other person shows that their trustworthy), the deeper the trust will go.

But, it's hard to trust the first time. And it's hard to evaluate trustworthiness. Because of that, many decide that it's easier to just not trust at all. It's definitely sad when a person chooses that route, but I think we can all understand why.

When you and I don't trust someone, it's very difficult to receive anything from them. Think about it, would you welcome a birthday gift from someone you don't trust? I would find myself thinking, "Why are they giving this to me? They must be up to something. They're probably going to use it to manipulate me or harm me in some way."

God invites all of us to trust him. But that can be hard. Often God can seem distant. Often God can seem silent. Often God can even seem untrustworthy. Just me? Ok.

However, every time I trust God, he comes through. It may not be how or even when I want Him to, but He does. And it's our trust in Him that gives us joy and peace. In other words, it doesn't come from what He does for us. It comes from this deep and abiding sense of trust in our good, good Father in Heaven who is our source of hope.

"Then," after you are filled with joy and peace because you trust Him, "then you will overflow with CONFIDENT hope through the power of the Holy Spirit." As we start a new week, I want to encourage you to overflow with confident hope this week through the power of the Holy Spirit. As a Pentecostal church, we believe that the power, work, and gift of the Holy Spirit is still at work today. Tap into that. Pray in your heavenly prayer language.

How are you on the trust scale? Do you find it easy or difficult to trust others (and God)? What is one step you can take this week to trust God?

Prayer: *"God, even if my actions and thoughts do not always show it, I trust you. I declare my trust in you today. I receive joy and peace from you, in Jesus' name. I open myself to the work and power of the Holy Spirit so that I may overflow with confident hope. In Jesus' name, amen."*

JOURNAL

DAY NINE

1 Corinthians 13:7 (NLT)
Love never gives up, never loses faith, is always hopeful, and endures through every circumstance.

I've said it before, but we use the word "love" in so many ways. I wish we had different words, like in the Greek language, that describe different types and levels of love. We don't. So, instead, we say we love our dog, we love our favorite restaurant, we love donuts, we love our spouse, we love our kids, and we love God. We also love our favorite color, our favorite movie, and our favorite season of the year.

Some of those are love. But many of them are just a strong affinity toward or a preference over some other option. It would be odd for me to say that I just have a strong affinity toward Consuela. Or I simply prefer my kids over someone else's. However, the opposite doesn't seem to be true. It's not weird at all for me to say I LOVE donuts!!

How do we know the difference? How do we differentiate between real love and our preferences?

Believe it or not, the answer is found in, among other things, HOPE.

True love never gives up. In other words, when something "better" comes along, I don't redirect my "love" from the old thing to the new thing. (That'll preach, won't it?)

True love never loses faith. My love is not dependent on how I feel, but on what I know is true. My faith in my wife, Consuela does not waiver simply because I feel down, discouraged, or distant. Why? Because I have faith that regardless of how I feel, she is the one for me. And, I have faith that she has my best interest in mind at all times and she is good, thoughtful, and caring toward me.

True love endures through every circumstance. There is no circumstance of life that will make me stop loving my kids. Even when they disappoint me, I will still love them the same. When they sin, I will still love them the same. When they don't live up to my expectations, I will still love them the same. Even when (if) they attack, reject, or offend me, I will still love them the same. My love for them endures through every circumstance.

True love is always hopeful. Because I love and am loved, I have hope. Hope and love are intimately connected. When you love others, you are infusing them with hope. When you bring hope to another, you are communicating to them that they are loved. When we feel the most hopeless are often the times when we feel the most un-loved or un-lovable.

Which of these characteristics of love come easiest to you? Which are the most difficult? What is one way to bring hope to another person today?

Prayer: *"God, I thank you for your amazing love toward me! Your love brings me hope every day! I pray that I will love people in a way that never gives up, deepens their faith, endures through everything, and brings hope. In Jesus' name, amen."*

JOURNAL

DAY TEN

1 Corinthians 13:13 (NLT)

Three things will last forever—faith, hope, and love—and the greatest of these is love.

It's hard to imagine that there is anything 'greater' than faith and hope. But, alas, there is! And for centuries, leaders (both inside and outside the church) have tried to convince us that faith and/or hope is the greatest. And while both are important, Paul, by the inspiration of the Holy Spirit, says very plainly to us all – no, no, no, LOVE is the greatest.

I am a huge basketball fan. Recently, there was a documentary airing on ESPN about Michael Jordan. And any time his name is brought into a conversation, the word G.O.A.T. is often mentioned. G.O.A.T. stands for "greatest of all time." Some think it's Michael Jordan. Others say Kareem, Bird, Magic, Kobe, or Lebron. Depending on the generation you find yourself in and perspective you have on the game, your answer can differ wildly from others.

I imagine that in Paul's time, there was some debate about which is the greatest. And arguments like that often come from a place of pride inside of us.

"Well, I'm really good at having faith and the Bible speaks of faith several times, so I must be the GOAT."

"I am always hopeful, and I can recite dozens of verses that talk about hope, so I must be the GOAT."

I often find that when I'm dealing with legalistic folks, they are legalistic about the things that come easy to them. They, of course, find a Scripture or two that backs up their argument, but it's based in what comes naturally to them. When identifying the GOAT, we must be careful to consider the breadth of Scripture and not just our own preferences.

And one last thing I want to draw your attention to here: faith and hope are internal and very difficult to quantify while love is external and can be seen, felt, and assessed by others. You see, God is supremely concerned with how we treat (love) one another. The foundation of the 10 commandments, for example, is how we treat (love) one another (and God). The "greatest commandment" is rooted in how we treat (love) one another (and God).

Couple that truth with the fact that faith and hope are intertwined with love so intimately that it's quite difficult to truly have faith or hope without love and it makes Paul admonition here all the more vivid for us today. So, it drives me to the point that I find myself at regularly – how well am I loving others? And, not just saying I love others, but actually showing I love others. And therein lies the answer to how well we're bringing hope to our community!

How well are you loving others – not just with words, but with actions?

Prayer: *"God, help me to love others with my words and actions. Help me to see opportunities today to show Your love to those around me. May I lift others up and give them hope through the love I extend toward them. In Jesus' name, amen."*

JOURNAL

DAY ELEVEN

1 Corinthians 15:19 (NLT)

And if our hope in Christ is only for this life, we are more to be pitied than anyone in the world.

As much as we all know that the things of this life are temporary, it can be hard to live that way, can't it? And I think the very delicate line that is being drawn here is not so much in pursuing the things we need, but rather in allowing the temporal things to define our levels of hope.

Put another way, when we do not get the things we want or even need, do we find ourselves feeling hopeless?

Taken a step further, in the context of this verse, if Jesus is only in your life to help you now and here, you are to be "pitied." And, when Jesus doesn't come through for you in the here and now, what happens to your hope is an indicator of whether you are to be pitied or not.

As Christians, we are always living for tomorrow (heaven) while impacting today (earth). We are to be salt and light here (earth) while having a trajectory toward there (heaven). God's desire is that we hope for Christ's redemption where we are (earth), while eagerly hoping for his final redemption when we will be gathered there (heaven). You see, it's not either/or, it's both/and.

There is more than this life. There is a Greater Reward. Heaven is real. If, as a follower of Jesus, we only see our relationship with Him as something to benefit us in this life, then we are to be pitied…and our hope in Christ is inadequate and insufficient.

In what ways can your hope in Christ increase more to include, not only this life, but the next?

Prayer: *"Father, I repent right now of the times that I have limited you in my view of who you are. I acknowledge right now that you are Christ for this life and the next. Help me to find the hope that is available to me because of Heaven. In Jesus' name, amen."*

JOURNAL

DAY TWELVE

Ephesians 1:18 (NLT)
I pray that your hearts will be flooded with light so that you can understand the confident hope he has given to those he called—his holy people who are his rich and glorious inheritance.

A few weeks ago, my daughter Victoria cleaned out our junk drawer at our house. Do you have a junk drawer at your house? Sure, you do. You may not call it that, but I would guess that there is some drawer, box, closet, or car where junk just seems to collect. And every now and then, you have to clean it out.

Did you know that our hearts can experience the same thing? Over time, our hearts can become cluttered with junk. And as more and more junk begins to pile on, the most important things can become hidden. Different than our junk drawers at home, when our hearts get this way, it can lead to major issues for us.

In order to know the hope of Jesus Christ, we need the junk cleared from our hearts. It's the light of Jesus that shines and illuminates truths about who He is. When our hearts are cluttered, it is easy to find yourself at a point of hopelessness.

The clutter in our hearts can come from what we watch, what we read, what we listen to, what we think about, what we put in our bodies, and so on. Each layer of junk only compounds the issues that we see and builds on the previous ones. We can easily imagine that we woke up one day distant from God and feeling hopeless and helpless, but in reality, it's happened over time – junk on top of junk on top of junk.

The remedy is two-fold. First, we must all take a regular inventory of what we're putting into our minds, hearts and bodies. Secondly, we must allow the Holy Spirit to examine us and point out any junk in our lives that needs removed. Then, we work in tandem with the Holy Spirit to address what has been revealed.

Pause right now and consider the potential junk you're putting into your heart. Also, allow the Holy Spirit to reveal to you what needs to be removed.

Prayer: *"God, I want to love you with all my heart. But, sometimes, I confess, I allow junk to clutter my heart. Please forgive me and show me what needs to be cleaned out. Give me the ability to address what needs to be removed so I can understand Your confident hope more. In Jesus' name, amen."*

JOURNAL

DAY THIRTEEN

Ephesians 2:12 (NLT)
In those days you were living apart from Christ. You were excluded from citizenship among the people of Israel, and you did not know the covenant promises God had made to them. You lived in this world without God and without hope.

Do you remember what life was like before you began a relationship Jesus? For some of us, we were young, so we lack the perspective of what we were saved from. For others, we were adults, so we understand fully what our lives were like without Him. Regardless of when we began a relationship with Him, we don't have to search far to know that life without Jesus is no life at all.

I want to invite you, for just a moment, to consider the many, many people who are far from Jesus today. Maybe there's a specific person that comes to mind that you're connected to who is lost. Maybe it's an unreached people group somewhere across the globe. Maybe it's a friend, a relative, a coworker, a child, or a neighbor.

Put plainly, those who do not have a relationship with Jesus are not just far from God, they're far from hope. And our mission, as stated by Jesus Himself, is to take the Good News to everybody. It's what we're doing, in essence, for this 21 Days of Hope. We're taking the Good News, that's so radically impacted our lives, to those around us.

And we do so, not just because Jesus said so, but because of the difference it's made for us. We know…we remember…the hopelessness of being far from God. We know…we remember…the pain of living apart from Christ. We know…we remember…the loneliness of being excluded from citizenship in Heaven.

If we truly know and remember these things, then our strongest response should be to act as vehicles of God's hope. We should be the conduit that He uses to reach a broken world. We should share about Jesus with the same amount of zeal that we are thankful for Jesus' work in us.

Have you shared about Jesus lately? If not, what could that look like for you today? Take a moment and journal about your salvation moment and use that as motivation to take the Good News to others.

Prayer: *"Father, I'm so thankful that I am a child of God. Thank you for bringing me out of hopelessness and despair into light and hope. Give me the courage to tell others about what I've found in a relationship with You. In Jesus' name, amen."*

JOURNAL

DAY FOURTEEN

1 Thessalonians 2:19 (NLT)
After all, what gives us hope and joy, and what will be our proud reward and crown as we stand before our Lord Jesus when he returns? It is you!

Paul writes this to the church in Thessalonica while being "quarantined" from them. They are separated from each other – to the point that he describes this "intense longing" to see each other again. How many of you would use those words to explain how you felt during the 2020 quarantine? I would guess, many of you.

Me too. Me too. My longing to see those I love grew more intense with each passing day.

In addition to a healthy, thriving relationship with Jesus Christ, it is true that we derive hope and joy from being with each other. I cannot wait until we are ALL gathered together worshiping our Father in Heaven and fellowshipping one with another.

But, I think Paul is describing something a little beyond just being together, don't you? Could it be that due to his reference to "our proud reward and crown as we stand before our Lord Jesus when he returns," he is talking about those we have personally led to Christ?

I think so.

It is another vivid reminder of our mission…of The Mission. That somehow our hope is little stronger, and our joy is little brighter each time someone steps across the line of salvation and says "yes" to making Jesus their Lord and Savior – because someone saw Jesus in us or heard about Him from us! I don't know about you, but I look forward to that day when Jesus says to me, "Well done, good and faithful servant!" And then I receive my proud reward and crown as I look around and see those I've somehow led to Christ!

Who's on your list? Who are those that need to hear about Jesus from you and see Jesus in you?

Prayer: *"Oh God, my prayer is simple today. I pray that you would use me. Open my eyes to see the opportunities around me. Give me the wisdom and confidence to lead someone else to you. In Jesus' name, amen."*

JOURNAL

DAY FIFTEEN

1 Thessalonians 4:13 (NLT)
And now, dear brothers and sisters, we want you to know what will happen to the believers who have died so you will not grieve like people who have no hope.

What are you grieving today? Perhaps Mother's Day is tough for you. Maybe you've lost a friend or loved one recently. Are you grieving missed opportunities due to the quarantine in 2020 like high school graduation, a family vacation, or birthday parties? Some are grieving broken marriages, empty bank accounts, and prodigal children.

Truth be told, we are probably all grieving something right now. It is natural to grieve. I regularly tell folks to be sure to grieve their losses fully and to navigate through the 5 stages of grief. Grief is a part of life and there is absolutely nothing wrong with grieving.

But, there is a difference for us as Christians. We do not grieve like others because, even when we grieve, we still have HOPE. And hope makes all the difference.

I have done countless funerals for people who have no relationship with Jesus. Funerals like those are different. They are far sadder. Family members are more distraught. The entire "feel" of the funeral is heavy and dark.

When I do a funeral for a believer, it is common that there is a sense of hope in the room. People are sad and somber, but there's just a difference in how they interact with me and others. I believe that's because they (we) have hope!

Hope changes things. Hope gives a new perspective. Hope helps us look beyond what we feel. Hope keeps us rooted in truth. Hope makes sense of the chaos and pain. Hope inspires us to keep going when we want to give up.

So, whatever you're grieving right now, have hope. Allow yourself the grace to grieve while keeping your eyes fixed on the One from who hope comes. And, when you can't find the hope you need, lean into others and allow their hope to fill you.

Prayer: *"God give me the strength to grieve well. May I find in the middle of my grief a hope that can only come from you. Hope for another day. Hope to believe (again). Hope that helps me find joy. In Jesus' name, amen."*

JOURNAL

DAY SIXTEEN

Titus 2:13 (NLT)

...while we look forward with hope to that wonderful day when the glory of our great God and Savior, Jesus Christ, will be revealed.

What are you looking forward to right now? For me, it's vacation. I desperately need a vacation. How about you? I'm not sure whether it's going to happen or not, but I am looking forward to it anyway.

For some of us, it's easy to look forward. While others of us, we are continually looking back. Still others, we are focused on what's going on right here, right now. Which one is best…or right?

I would submit that all 3 of them are right – with balance.

We should look back. We should remember what Jesus did on the cross. We should remember where came from. We should look back to see how far we've come and how much Jesus has done in our lives.

We should focus on the present. We should be present for our families and our friends. We shouldn't be caught up in regrets of the past or looking ahead toward some "what if" tomorrow. We should be fully present seeing all that God is doing in us and through us today.

We should also look forward to the future. Among many other things, we should be looking forward to Christ's return. Why? Because unlike other things that we may be looking forward to, this one is assured. Because of that, it goes beyond a dream or a goal and becomes something worthy of our hope.

What does "looking forward" to Christ's return look like for you? How can it become a source of hope, especially right now?

Prayer: *"Heavenly Father, there are so many things that I look forward to. I recognize that some will happen, and some won't. Today, I choose to look forward to Jesus' return – the one thing that is sure to happen. Thank you for the hope that brings my life. In Jesus' name, amen."*

JOURNAL

DAY SEVENTEEN

Hebrews 6:11 (NLT)
Our great desire is that you will keep on loving others as long as life lasts, in order to make certain that what you hope for will come true.

Love others as long as life lasts. It's connected to your hope. And don't just say you love others, actually show love to others.

Who can you love today (that you wouldn't have normally "loved")?

Write their name(s):

_____

_____

_____

_____

Prayer: *"God, help me to love others as Jesus did. In His name, amen."*

JOURNAL

DAY EIGHTEEN

Hebrews 6:19 (NLT)

This hope is a strong and trustworthy anchor for our souls. It leads us through the curtain into God's inner sanctuary.

Perhaps lately you've felt like you've been tossed back and forth by the waves of circumstances that have been coming at you. You've perhaps found it difficult to find your footing in our "new normal." Or you've been eager to see things return to normal.

As I talk with people, it has become clear to me that there are folks on both ends of the spectrum and everywhere in between. Very few of us, however, have found ourselves on a smooth and steady trajectory forward (me included). The things we interact with have the potential to put all of us, in one way or another and whether we recognize it or not, in the middle of a storm.

For some of us, the waves have been high and are crashing hard. For others, they have been little waves with just a little effect. For some, the waves are coming frequently and non-stop while others are experiencing waves intermittently.

Even with the differences of our experiences and temperaments with regard to the quarantine, one truth holds steady – God is our hope, and that hope is our anchor!

And when we allow our hope in God to be our anchor, we will experience God's presence at new and exciting depths. As much as I would love to tell you that experiencing God's presence comes easy for us, I cannot. I have found that the deepest times that I've experienced God have been through struggles and storms. But the choice is ours. He is available to be found, but we must look for Him.

How are you feeling today? Please send me a message to let me know how you're doing and how I can pray for you!

Prayer: *"Thank you, God, for the hope that comes only from You. Help me to look to you, alone, when I find myself in the storms of life. I pray that I will experience the inner sanctuary over and over again. In Jesus' name, amen."*

JOURNAL

DAY NINETEEN

Hebrews 10:23 (NLT)
Let us hold tightly without wavering to the hope we affirm, for God can be trusted to keep his promise.

In 2010, there was a storm that rolled through the city I was living in. My oldest son, Samuel, wasn't very old. And on the outside of his bedroom wall a piece of siding had come loose and was banging loudly. He was crying and couldn't fall back asleep.

Being the heroic dad that I was, I sprang into action! I got my coat on and grabbed the ladder. As I climbed to the top of the ladder to pull the loose piece of siding off, the wind began to blow stronger and stronger. I ripped the siding off…and then I felt the ladder begin to fall.

Using quick thinking, I jumped from the top rung of the ladder to the ground so that I wouldn't come crashing down to the ground. But…as I landed on the ground, my ankle gave way under me. I'm guessing it just couldn't hold the weight. I rolled my ankle and over the next 24 hours it began to swell. Nothing was broken, but I was in severe pain for several days. I still have pain there every now and then.

The ladder was supposed to hold me. The ladder was supposed to stand strong and lift me to the place I needed to go. The ladder was the means to my heroic fatherhood! But it failed me. I put my trust in the ladder and it let me down.

Aren't you glad that God is nothing like this ladder? I know I am. He is always trustworthy. He will always do what He says He'll do. He will keep all His promises!

In fact, I think we are kind of like the ladder, aren't we? We waver. We get blown over. We don't hold up against the things coming at us. We are nothing like God. Isn't it good to recognize that from time to time?

In what areas of your life are you wavering right now? Find one Scripture that contains a promise from God that can help you trust Him more.

Prayer: *"Father God, I am so thankful that you can be trusted. That you will keep all your promises. Forgive me for the times I've wavered. Help me to trust you in every situation. In Jesus' name, amen."*

JOURNAL

DAY TWENTY

Hebrews 11:1 (NLT)
Faith shows the reality of what we hope for; it is the evidence of things we cannot see.

We have one more day left, after today, of our 21 Days of Hope. I sincerely HOPE that these devotionals have infused your days with hope (see what I did there?). Now we can look forward to what the future has in store for us!

But the truth is, we don't know what tomorrow holds. We can't see beyond our current circumstances, can we? For those of us that like to control our lives, that can be a scary thought! But I'll say it again, that's where hope and faith intertwine.

Our hope is placed in the unseen. And that is the essence of faith. Our faith is to be firmly in place regardless of how things look. Although our faith can feel like (and look like) a roller coaster sometimes, the goal is for it to level out more and more as we trust God more.

Have you ever had someone throw you a surprise birthday party? I have.

On that day, it feels like it's just going to be another birthday. You do all the stuff you have done every other year. Your family sings to you, you blow out the candles, you open some presents, you eat some cake. And there's nothing wrong with that, right?

When there's a surprise birthday party planned for you, nothing LOOKS different. By all appearances, it's just another birthday. You go about your day with the expectation that everything is normal and you're going to lay your head down that night after experiencing the standard birthday.

Then, BOOM! You walk into a restaurant, a room, your house, even – and there stands a big group of family, friends, and acquaintances yelling "HAPPY BIRTHDAY!!" If you're an extrovert, it's the best feeling in the world. If you're an introvert, it can be a little scary and overwhelming (although it's appreciated no less than an extrovert).

What happens is that all in a moment, you are blessed beyond belief. You're surprised. You're elated. You're excited. You didn't SEE it coming! By the way things looked, you never would have guessed it.

And I think that's what this verse is saying. Your days are meant to be good, like a birthday. And there's nothing wrong with that. But every now and then, God shows up and shows out and you are blessed beyond belief. In that moment, you are confidently certain that God loves you. And the hope and faith you have has been confirmed (or evidenced).

When was the last time God showed up and threw you a surprise "birthday party"?

Prayer: *"God, help me to have faith despite what I see happening around me. I pray that my hope in You will help me through the difficult times. Give me the perspective to persevere through the everyday and recognize the times you show up and surprise me. In Jesus' name, amen."*

JOURNAL

DAY TWENTY-ONE

1 Peter 3:15 (NLT)

Instead, you must worship Christ as Lord of your life. And if someone asks about your hope as a believer, always be ready to explain it.

Most Sundays, we gather together as the Church and we worship. It is often a reminder of who (or what) we are worshiping. It can be easy to find ourselves worshiping lots of things other than God, can't it? I mean, we're not singing songs about it or bowing down in front of it. But we can all too often, with honest reflection, discover that there are things we are worshiping in place of God.

And the world is watching. The world around us – our neighbors, coworkers, friends, and family – they see very clearly our worship. Are we truly worshipers of God or something else? A world that is so desperately searching for hope, they are looking for an authentic expression of worship from us.

Instead, I worry that we worship politicians and political rhetoric far more than we worship God. I worry that we worship our jobs and the money that we have far more than we worship God. I worry that we worship relationships, addictions, our children, and even our own comfort far more than we worship God. And the people around us see it.

I want to challenge all of us on this final day of our 21 Days of Hope to evaluate who, or what, we worship. And not just a casual evaluation, but one that is critical and sincere.

When times are tough, where do I turn first?
When someone offends me, what is my first step to resolve it?
When I am stressed and anxious, who is the one I talk to most?
When things seem uncertain or chaotic, how do I make sense of it?
When I experience a blessing, through what lens do I view it?
When I am being stretched and challenged to grow, how do I react?
Would a person who is not a Christian see HOPE in me when I'm faced with the above-mentioned scenarios?

The world is watching. And it is my sincere desire that the people in your circle of influence will see HOPE in you to such a level that they must ask you, "Why?" and that you and I will "always be ready to explain it."

Spend some time reflecting, in prayer, on the questions above and allow the Holy Spirit to speak to you today.

JOURNAL

OTHER BOOKS:

Equipping the Warrior: 75 Leadership Devotions for Men

Equipping the Warrior brings together 13 authors who explore the roles and responsibilities of today's man. This spiritual dive comes in the form of shared experiences and wisdom to help men step into the roles of father, brother, warrior!

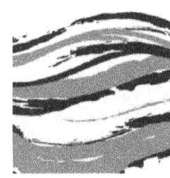

The Journey: A 40-Day Devotional for Spiritual Health

We are all on a journey. As Christians, we should be on a path toward growing in maturity and becoming more and more like Christ. The Journey 40-Day Devotional covers four areas of spiritual growth:

- *Having a correct view of God*
- *Giving spiritual growth ongoing attention*
- *Trust God more*
- *Engaging in spiritual exercise*

If you're ready to take steps to become more spiritually healthy, this devotional is for you! Each day includes questions to consider, a prayer prompt, and space to journal about what you've read. This devotional is for the new, intermediate, or experienced Christian! Everyone will benefit from the intentional journey it takes the reader through.

Find these and more at www.timparsons.me

www.ingramcontent.com/pod-product-compliance
Lightning Source LLC
Chambersburg PA
CBHW071408040426
42444CB00009B/2145